Stroking the Compulsion

Workaholism

by

Bill Smith

authorHOUSE®

AuthorHouse™
1663 Liberty Drive, Suite 200
Bloomington, IN 47403
www.authorhouse.com
Phone: 1-800-839-8640

First published by AuthorHouse 10/23/2007

ISBN: 978-1-4343-2591-4 (sc)

Library of Congress Control Number: 2007933646

Printed in the United States of America
Bloomington, Indiana

This book is printed on acid-free paper.

PREFACE

This book is written as an inspiration for hope to all those workaholics who survive in an unknowing manner of being a workaholic each day at the expense of damaging the relationships with their family and friends.

This book is written in the male orientation, as there is a much greater likelihood of male workaholics than female, however in each instance that reference is given to gender, the opposite gender may equally apply to the situation.

There are not many support groups in the United States to help the workaholic. Though there are some books written on the subject of workaholism, for me they were not much help. This is a true story of my life experience with workaholism. I have now lost two (2) families through divorce because of my disease. There is not true supportive help in our society for a workaholic. If you are a workaholic, and have a family life that is whole, I truly applaud your success. If you are a workaholic who has a family life that has been shattered, you are not alone.

The writer wishes to express his gratitude to contributing writers - Jane Waters and Ann Lindsey who assisted with their technical expertise on certain chapters of the book. Both are licensed therapists working with families, and dealing both directly and indirectly with the results of effects of workaholics.

It is also interesting to note that as this book is being final edited in May 2007, the latest versions of word processing programs still do not include "workaholic" or "workaholism" in their spell checker - perhaps supportive of the thoughts presented throughout the book.

Finally, I want you to know why the book is set out in the format you will see. I have double spaced the lines to allow you to use this book as a "workbook" while reading. I have also only printed the pages on one side. This will allow you, the reader, to write your own thoughts in the spaces provided as you read this book, perhaps to evaluate your own life as a workaholic, or to determine if you may have workaholic tendencies.

May God Bless You and Keep You, May He Wrap HIS Arms Around You, and Give You Peace.

DEDICATION

Though the writing of this book began as a project solely by myself, my ex-wife (Janey) and her colleague (Ann) who are both family therapist. It was initiated as a project of recovery for me. I will share many intimate moments and feelings with the reader throughout the book, again as a part of my 12-Step Recovery Program. I do this in humility, trusting in my Higher Power that the words which are written will help someone else in their recovery, or to help someone recognize that they may be a workaholic, or in a relationship with a workaholic.

I dedicate this book to my third wife, Vernessa, whose love, caring, and support, along with the power of God, has changed my live forever.

My family has been through many difficult times as a result of the behaviors which I exhibit as a workaholic in everyday life. I truly appreciate their support and love for me in my temporary recovery and backsliding processes. I hope they will always be with me either in mind or in Spirit through the rest of our lives together and separate.

I DEDICATE THIS BOOK TO MY WIFE VERNESSA, MY
SONS, ADAM AND JESSE
and
TO MY DAUGHTER, NIKI
ALL OF WHOM I LOVE WITH ALL MY HEART

Contents

<u>Notes</u>

Chapter 1 - Definition

Workaholism is a term that describes the process of being addicted to work. It creates a profound loss of control of his or her own environment.

We are not saying that working hard is a sin or that it is not an admirable trait, nor are we saying that working hard occasionally is not warranted. On the contrary, many fields require an intermittent fast paced, high productivity period. We are not referring to people who turn to work mainly to avoid intimacy, responsibility, conflict, or boredom, even though the result of workaholism is the same. We are making a distinction between the <u>hard</u> worker and the <u>compulsive</u> worker. In U.S. News and World Report, April 7, 1986, industrial psychologist David Sirota is quoted in an article as saying that "A normal healthy person has three aspects to life: Work, play, and love." The <u>compulsive</u> worker does not have a balanced life that includes those elements. The addicted person does not have that choice, nor is he in control of that aspect. In another article entitled, "When Work Becomes An Obsession," published in Utne Reader, July/August 1988, Fred Moody described such a man. Moody reported that Robert McFarlane, Reagan's former National Security Adviser, 'had allowed his work "to become

<u>Notes</u>

almost the exclusive measure of my worth."' Moody further reports that McFarlane, dominated by a stern father who was taught to hide his emotions and strive for success at all costs, grew up "to become a classic workaholic - an emotionally withdrawn person for whom success in the workplace is the sole reason for being. When he failed - as inevitably happens to all perfectionists - McFarlane fell into a suicidal depression." In the same article, Moody quotes psychiatrist Wayne Katon, a specialist in depression who frequently treats alcoholics, as saying that most workaholics believe, often unconsciously, that they will not be loved for who they are, only for what they produce. Further, those workaholics feel a sense of loneliness, seeking admiration, but are never fulfilled because admiration is not the same thing as love.

Workaholism has the same qualities as any other addiction or compulsion. It affects the social, emotional, spiritual, and physical aspects of the addicted person. Though we will discuss these aspects in more detail later, we will briefly describe its effects now.

Workaholism can affect the social realm of the addicted person by interfering with close personal relationships, among family members and friends. The more the workaholic turns to work, the more resentful family members become. The more that people come to rely on the workaholic, the more they will be disappointed, leaving them angry, hurt, and neglected. The more negative feelings the workaholic encounters from close relationships, the more likely the workaholic will retreat deeper into work. This becomes a downward spiraling pattern which

Notes

will gradually destroy close relationships, as long as the concept of workaholism as a disease is not fully understood.

Workaholism affects the emotional aspect of the addicted person by bringing with it conditions such as clinical depression, anxiety disorders, or paranoia. Frequently the workaholic will turn to other addictions, such as drugs, alcohol, compulsive overeating, to mask the pain felt by themselves as a result of not feeling able to control their lives or relationships.

Workaholism affects the spiritual realm of the addicted person by allowing the workaholic to become spiritually bankrupt. The further advanced the person has become in the progression of his addiction, the more distant he feels from God or a Higher Power. The workaholic begins to feel that there is less good in the world and fewer caring, loving people, partially because they are in so much emotional pain, and partially due to the very real possibility that those around them have become less loving and less caring toward the workaholic. The workaholic doubts the very existence of these concepts because pain has interfered with the ability to love or be loved. The shame cycle pattern begins to form: the less the workaholics feel loved, the less they show love, the less they feel worthy of being loved, so they act in an uncaring way toward others due to lowered self-esteem and pain, so others will show them less love because of the way they have acted. This pattern continues unless interrupted by a recovery program.

Lastly, workaholism affects the addicted person in the area of physical health. Because of the above problems and patterns

6

Notes

in their lives, they may experience a wide range of physical symptoms such as ulcers, migraines, backaches, extreme muscle pain, high blood pressure, and other stress related symptoms. They may be more subject to colds, flu and other common illnesses, and may experience direct effects from other addictive behaviors of smoking or drug and alcohol abuse.

Workaholism, having the same equalities and affects as other addictions, also follows the disease pattern that are common to recognized addictions. Workaholism is a disease, just like alcoholism, that affects not only the individual, but the entire family. There are many factors that make workaholism a disease.

The first factor is symptoms. These are recognizable behaviors and stages that can be diagnosed. Those who know what to look for can easily see workaholism in action.

The second factor is predictability. This means that the disease follows a certain course and patterns can be predicted.

Third, the disease is primary, meaning it is of first importance. The person must be treated for this and any other addictions first, before any progress can be made for any other concerns, like depression.

The fourth factor is that the disease is progressive. If left untreated, the disease will always get worse in all aspects of the person's life - emotionally, spiritually, physically, and socially.

Notes

The fifth factor in the disease determination is that it be chronic. Once it is present, it will always be there, and there is no known cure.

Yet, for the sixth factor, the disease is treatable. Even though there is no cure, like diabetes, there is potential for a successful and long lasting remission.

The last factor is the fatality of the disease. If the workaholic is left untreated, or does not change the course of the disease in some way, he or she will die a premature death, either physically or emotionally, given that it will have progressed to its most advanced stage.

Notes

Chapter 2 - Identification of a Workaholic

Workaholism is a progressive disease in which there are basically four stages. The first is the learning phase. A person, who may inevitably become a workaholic, is just newly experiencing the action of working hard and experiencing the benefits of working hard. This person usually receives positive, supportive consequences, such as respect from co-workers; support from family; maybe an increase in salary or a substantial bonus; or more company benefits or perks; all of which cause him no pain and the family members directly benefit from the recognition of the person. Many people function at this level. After the "working hard" period is over, the person returns to a normal, less hectic schedule, mainly feeling tired, but feeling good.

The second stage is the seeking phase. The person takes the knowledge learned and experiences and rewards from the first phase and applies it more often. Even though the person may turn to work more often, he will only work at appropriate places or times. The working hard time will not be considered as excessive, nor will it cause himself or anyone else pain. The person will seek work as an outlet or distraction for awhile. The workaholic is still deriving benefits from hard work and

Notes

will seek out times to do so, even when not at the place of business. If "work" was "alcohol" at this stage, people would be known as "social drinkers" or "recreational" drug users. The person controls himself by rules of his own about when to work and when to stop. It is important to know that the person is still in control of those decisions at this stage.

The third stage in this progressive illness is the "harmful dependency phase". This is when the person loses sight of self-imposed rules about when and where to work. The person will start to work during times that are inappropriate (i.e. on vacations, during designated family activities, in bed in the evening, while waiting for his wife to give birth to their baby in the hospital or while waiting for her husband to complete a heart bypass operation). The workaholic may not recognize that he is compromising his values and what he believes in, like missing a son's baseball games because of work, or missing a wedding anniversary dinner because of working late. At this phase, family problems begin to arise and the focus tends to center on the workaholic and his working patterns. For some, their behavior, in conflict with their values, may lead them to feel very negatively about themselves, knowing that they are disappointing and hurting family members. Other workaholics may not recognize any of these conflicts and wonder what is going on with family members. All aspects in the workaholic's own life will begin to suffer. Their relationships with family and friends will become strained and painful. The workaholic will experience emotional pain from guilt about his behavior, the pressure from bosses to work harder, or paranoid about job security. Because of the power that working has over his life,

Notes

the workaholic's values and morals will decline as his behavior shows preference for work over his family and friends. He begins to lie about how he "must go to this meeting", so he'll have to miss his daughter's play at school; and he will begin to experience physical symptoms of stress as he tries to handle this deterioration (i.e. headaches, backaches, tightening of neck muscles, stomachaches, frequent illnesses, etc.) but will still go to work. There will usually be a double message to the family now: he will say that the family is his preference, but his behavior will say that work is his preference.

The last stage of dependency is the "using-to-feel-normal phase". Now the workaholic stays in such a state of readiness and pressure, there is little time for fun, play, relaxation, or unwinding. The addicted person has now lost control of how long he will work and where he will work. This feeling of powerlessness over his own life and the fact that his life has become so unmanageable will cause him to feel enormous pressure, most of which he will try to deny or repress. The person works for any reason, but mainly to avoid the pain or the complaining at home. At this stage there comes little relief from all the pain that has so interfered in his life from all directions. The person only feels "normal" when he is working. If this process is not reversed, the person will die from stress induced illnesses (i.e. heart attack, etc.).

Our readers should understand that this disease can be treated at any of these phases. It does not need to get to the most advanced stage before changes can be made.

Notes

Description of a Workaholic

There is a real difference when an individual stops working hard and begins to be addicted to work. The workaholic's mind thinks of nothing but work. It is a very obsessive behavior. For the reader's benefit, I will try to create a composite profile of a workaholic using myself at various stages in my most addictive times, prior to initiating a recovery program. If any of this description sounds familiar, then maybe your family situation is not as good as it could be and perhaps there is a need for some change in your life.

Since I seem to be on a merry-go-round that never stops, I will begin in the morning, though that may be in the middle of a workaholic's thought patterns. Trying to stay in bed in the morning, whether it is a weekday or a weekend is next to impossible. From the moment of that first realization that another day has begun, I must be up and going. I usually try to begin planning my day, sometimes with a written list, but certainly with a mental review of the day, week and possibly month upcoming, for both the workplace activities and the home requirements. My eating habits are not as good as they should be, I usually have juice and maybe fruit. It takes too long to prepare and eat a full breakfast - there's stuff to do.

As the rest of the family begins to rise, I'm already moving in full gear and expect those sleepyheads to catch up in an instant. Their delays in getting ready begin to raise the stress level internally - the muscles begin to tighten in the neck and the need for control by shouting instruction begins. The family

Notes

may desire to sit and have a nice family-oriented breakfast and discuss dreams or allow the morning to creep upon them slowly. Here comes the workaholic like "a bull in the china shop" being disruptive and trying to get everyone in high gear again. Times a wastin', need to get to work and school so productive behaviors can begin (there's no soft side for the workaholic). The workaholic needs to finish the daily schedule - Morning work, Quick lunch, Afternoon work break -maybe, Return to home, Evening meal, After dinner work (inside/ outside/office work), Bedtime exhausted - no time for family, spouse, relaxation, thoughts, sitting/reading/discussing etc. Then start all over the next day.

<u>Notes</u>

Chapter 3 - "What's Your Style?"

We have found there are several different types of workaholics, not just one category into which all workaholics fit. In our studies we have become aware of three distinct categories. These are, but not limited to, the "Professional in the Corporation", the "Non-prioritizer", and the "Housewife" workaholics.

Professional in the Corporation

The first category of workaholic is the one most commonly recognized. When anyone mentions the term "workaholic", most people think of the "Professional in the Corporation." This is typically a middle to upper class income person working in a respected middle to upper management position. There can certainly be variations as to the type of corporation; as it can be a large, medium, or small business. Typically, it is the man who is the workaholic, but more and more we are observing the introduction of the woman in this category as well. These workaholics are usually the ones who come in to work before work hours begin and who stay late into the evening; long after everyone else has gone home. They work through lunch, seeing no reason for taking a break and who deny their own need for one. They usually seem to find businesses or

Notes

jobs that actually foster workaholism. They are seldom at home because they are working or traveling "in the name of business". When they are at home, they are seldom "present in mind", so the family feels they may as well be away from home anyway. These workaholics often miss dinners with the family and any after school activities in which their children are involved. When they are present for dinner at home, they're often lost in thoughts of work. They will get irritated if anyone interrupts their thoughts. For the most part, they just want to be left alone when they arrive home. They always bring work home and believe they "must" do several hours worth of work every night. Sometimes you'll find these workaholics up at odd hours in the night, when everyone is sleeping, because they're either thinking about work or actually doing work. One man quotes, "There's a creative thought which I must put down on paper before I lose it with another creative thought of work." The workaholic usually carries great enthusiasm and energy about their work, often to the point where little energy and time is left, and not intentionally saved, for family or their own personal interests, if they still have either left in their lives.

Non-Prioritizer

The second category of workaholic we call the "Non-prioritizer". This type of workaholic has a very difficult time distinguishing what activities must be performed and what activities can wait for a later time. They can neither tell the difference between the essential and the non-essential tasks, either at work or at home, nor prioritize the tasks into those that must be completed. To these workaholics every task has equal weight. The non-

Notes

prioritizer usually doesn't get any task completed because there are so many tasks to perform. Though they may start many tasks, they will rarely finish any of them. Since they leave so much incomplete in their lives, they usually end up feeling either unsatisfied or dissatisfied with their performance.

Most of the tasks being performed by the non-prioritizer are really non-essential. An example of a non-prioritizer's list of things to do is as follows:

- Rearranging the living room furniture
- Reorganizing the study desk drawers
- Sharpening all his tools
- Fixing the kitchen cabinet drawers
- Getting more envelopes
- Checking the lawn equipment
- and the list goes on and on

Since these types of workaholics can't prioritize, they find it difficult to begin any task. If they don't begin a task, they don't feel an accomplishment. If they begin a task but don't finish, they still feel little accomplishment. If they do complete some tasks there is a sense of good feeling, but this is only short-lived because they realize that they are accomplishing some non-essential tasks that generally have no importance. Non-prioritizers will have endless lists of tasks that need to be completed. They focus so intensely on the myriad of projects that "must" be completed that it quickly leads them to being overwhelmed. This overwhelming feeling leads to a general feeling of being totally out of control. The projects and lists

Notes

have taken on a life and energy of their own. To control their fear of being overwhelmed, the non-prioritizer will intensely concentrate on just one thing, to the exclusion of all other people and tasks.

These tasks may not be important to non-workaholics, but they serve an important function for these non-prioritizer workaholics. They do all of this to control their fear and to consume time and psychological energy. This initiates their addiction of "having to do all these tasks". There is a loss of control over this thinking and acting which leads to a sense of isolation from loved ones, and lowers their already deteriorating self-esteem. There is no validation of their self-worth or of their loved ones because they are too caught up in the intensity of trying to perform so many tasks.

Housewife

The third category of workaholics is the "Housewife". We felt that even though this category has similarities to the "Profession in the Corporation" and the "Non-Prioritizer," it really deserves its own category. This is usually, though not always, a woman who feels primarily responsible for the typical housewife duties, and is caretaker of the home. As we all know, housework is never finished. There is always one more thing that needs to be completed. If there are children in the home, the feeling is worse because parenting is never completed either. There is always the costume to make for the child's play, the button to sew on her dress, another load of laundry to do, ashtrays to be emptied and cleaned, one more bill to pay, dishes to be washed,

<u>Notes</u>

lunches to be made, clothes to be picked up, and the list goes on and on. The housewife workaholic will be constantly tending to these details to the exclusion of her spouse and children. Trying to get her attention for a conversation is a chore, so no one ever really gets her full attention. The family receives a message from the housewife workaholic that they are not important as the cleaning or the dusting. A typical question that arises from the family in this household is, "When is it my turn?" The family asks this question because they seldom get the opportunity to be with "Mom". The woman workaholic may eventually ask this same question because she never feels she gets time for herself either. This woman so deeply feels the compulsion to keep working that she cannot stop herself from constantly tending to the details of the household.

Notes

Chapter 4 - Who Enable Workaholism?

To support our belief that certain types of people enable workaholism, we turned to many articles, one of which is entitled, "Hooked on Work", by Anne Wilson Schaef and Diane Fassel. The authors write that "equally important in the addictive system are the co-dependents, those who consciously or not, support and encourage the addict's self-destructive behavior - who, rather than tell the truth, choose to say the "nice things" or "look the other way". The authors further report that "without co-dependents, addicts could not survive".

Society, as a whole, promotes workaholism. More specifically, though, the "Corporation", family, and friends promote this socially acceptable addition. Nationally syndicated columnist Colman McCarthy was quoted in the article, "Workaholism: No Life for the Leisurelorn?" by Edward R. Walsh as saying, "The workaholic's way of life is considered in America to be at one and the same time a religious virtue, a form of patriotism, the way to win friends and influence people and the way to be healthy, wealthy, and wise. Therefore, the workaholic, plagued though he be, is unlikely to change. Why? Because his is a sort of paragon of virtue. He is chosen as the one most likely to succeed." Society holds workaholism as far

Notes

more a <u>virtue</u> than a <u>vise</u>, is a belief shared by many authors and therapists in the addiction fields. The author of "When Work Becomes and Obsession: in the Utne Reader says, "The person who works right up to the point of self-destruction is often accorded far more esteem than the person who seeks to lead a balanced life." He further reports that there is a real "pressure to work at the expense of our physical health and the health of relationships."

One of the major institutions in society that actually fosters workaholism is the "Corporation". Companies promote workaholism because, logically, it is seemingly, in their best interest, financially. The Corporation feeds on itself by having more people burn the midnight oil. At first, that would be true, but then the price of burnout and inefficiency would set in. In her article, "Workaholic Managers Create Stagnant DP Shop", Brenda Moss writes that the tendency towards workaholism is especially great in the computer field. She believes, further, that workaholic managers fail to communicate well with their staff. These people initially worked in data processing, which is basically a solitary occupation, and one not needing communication skills on a daily basis. These workaholic managers create work where it doesn't exist, and assume everyone else in the office should be kept as busy as the workaholic. Even if the manager doesn't actually say those words, there is usually the assumption being made by those working around him that they <u>should</u> be as busy by following his actions as their leader or supervisor.

Notes

Workaholism can also be reflected in personnel evaluations. The workaholic supervisor evaluates his employees on a basis equivalent to his own performance, rather than the norm. Anyone who has a workaholic boss will tell you that it is stressful around the office most of the time when he's there. Usually the workers are relieved when he's away because things are less hectic, less chaotic, and everyone is less irritable. Expectations by the workaholic boss, who often is also a perfectionist, are unrealistically high. The workaholic boss and the worker who report to him know that those expectations cannot be continuously met. Thus, there is a pervasive feeling of failure among the workers, and a feeling that nothing they could do would ever satisfy the manager. Under this pressure, the workers' motivation usually decreases, as well as job performance. Yet, the workers will usually say nothing about their feelings, sometimes because of fear, but mainly because of their co-dependent, people-pleasing personalities. So, the worker enable the workaholic manager by accepting the mood swings of the workaholic manager, and suppressing their own feelings. Thus, a system is established which will continue the circle of unhealthy relationships and dysfunctional working conditions.

Not only do co-workers enable workaholism to flourish, but most corporate structures often thrive on the addiction. In the article, "Management by Stress", authors Mike Parker and Jane Slaughter describe a company that uses stress as its style of management. This company believes that "personal stress as well as system stress drives production." They believe stress gets the most profit from its labor force. By

Notes

operating the system, assembly line work for example, under a state of permanent, constant stress, they identify both weak and strong points, indicating where changes may need to be made to obtain maximum performance from their employees. This company uses chimes and lights that quickly identify the specific worker who is not keeping up with expected production. Those who don't keep up on the line are fired. The authors then say that "the only solution is to keep up, no matter what it takes" and I would believe it would be at <u>all</u> costs. It was reported that most workers don't use their break periods to re-strengthen themselves or for meeting their socializing needs. Most workers, it is reported, use that time to catch up on the production they missed or to get ahead of the required production goals. Using this system of management, though, whatever was produced would still not be good enough. The workers probably strive to surpass even the highest levels of productivity met. If the employees are compulsive workers themselves, they would be unaware of their own limits. We can only imagine the toll this stress would take on a worker if this level of pressure continued day after day. The company justifies this type of management saying that they get high productivity figures, and they get this "from pushing employees to work overtime for free."

In reviewing the above situation, most people will be appalled at the behavior of the company. It is easy to blame that company and to want to make them the "bad guys". But it must be explained in terms of enabling behavior. Each side shares equal responsibility for allowing this type of personal stress to continue. The company could look at what they are

<u>Notes</u>

asking of their employees to do in terms of financial values and productivity. The workers could ask themselves why they are willing to be treated in such an abusive manner, while continuing to say nothing. Each party cannot exist without the other party. Yet neither party will indicate where their limits are, and probably have denied their feelings for so long that they don't realize they even have or deserve limits. The price, of course, is emotional and/or physical death for the individual. If the workers stay in these circumstances while experiencing these conditions, then they are doing what Anne Wilson Schaef and Diane Fassel described in "Hooked on Work". They write, "When loyalty to the organization becomes a substitute for one's own life, then the company has become the substance of choice."

There are certain signs that are quite indicative of an addictive organization or the Corporation which fosters workaholism. There is usually a high rate of turnover in these Corporations. Many employees experience burnout, while those that are still in control of themselves will quit or ask to be reassigned. The cost of retraining has a tremendous impact on the financial balance sheet, if properly accounted. In addition, schedule delays and disruptions of project teams creates negative motivation. It can also be noticed that the executives in the Corporation are forced beyond their creative powers. As a consequence, very few positive results are being obtained or created at this level. The price of health is being paid for by workaholism. The Corporation can expect to see a rise in stress-related illnesses (i.e. heart attacks, ulcers, high blood pressure, etc.) If further probed into the workaholic' personal

Notes

life, you'll find problems with marriage, and the relationship with the workaholic's children as a direct result of the work addition. These problems may show up in the forms of drug/ alcohol abuse, eating disorders, mental health disorders, and school failure, to name a few.

If a Corporation fosters workaholism, or is addicted itself, it can also be detected in the benefits' package. Again, we agree with the authors of "Hooked on Work" with regards to benefits. The authors write that benefits are an important and necessary factor. But, "the issue is not of the benefits per se, but the way the organization uses them to stay central in the lives of workers and to prevent workers from moving on and doing what they need to do. When the benefits become a controlling factor in a person's life, the organization becomes the addictive agent. It is when the organization is willing to take advantage of the worker's dependence and to be competitive with other work places for the worker's loyalty and creativity that the organization functions as the addictive agent." Sick leave and vacation or comp time can provide clues about the organization's addiction or enabling status, or the individual's workaholism. We can expect a significant amount of unused sick leave or bonuses given to employees for not taking sick leave. We can look a their policies on vacation. How little is given and is there incentive pay for those days not taken? Is there a tremendous amount of comp time being put in by employees without retrieval? A look a the individual worker's records of these benefits can provide clues. Not only will we see a significant amount of unused vacation time and sick leave, but we can note how many employees leave a telephone number

Notes

where they can be reached while on vacation; how often the employee checks in with the Corporation while vacationing; how may employees take work with them while on vacation; and how many employees return early from vacation because they can't stay away from work any longer. All of these are good indicators of whether there is addiction and/or enabling present.

There are two levels of employees within the Corporation that display enabling behaviors. One is upper level management. These are the policy makers of the organization. The policies reflect the presence of workaholism as an addiction, whether the policy makers themselves are addicted or whether they are enabling workaholism to continue with their employees. Some corporations have a policy where a promotion is based upon the amount of money generated for the Corporation per person. This is reflected in billable hours. The policy makers often have unwritten expectations regarding how often the employees stay late, how often they come in on weekends, and how often they take work home. Even though these unwritten rules cannot be enforced, there is often an enormous amount of pressure being placed on the employees to conform to these working conditions. Upper management also controls the benefits that are provided, or are not provided, based on factors stated above relating to the employee's performance, even if the worker's performance appraisals are exemplary.

The other level of employees in a corporation that fosters workaholism is mid-level management. These are the policy **enforcers** of the Corporation. These employees are the ones

Notes

who set the example of all the expectations listed above. They have the unfortunate situation of being caught in a double bind. They are close enough to the workers they supervise to know their needs and working conditions, yet are also aware of the Corporation's needs and financial status. Mid-level management tries to change policies and procedures to best fit both sides, but are inhibited by time constraints and pressures from upper level management to get more work out of the employees.

A second category of people who enable workaholism is the family of the workaholic. The spouse usually assumes responsibility for the workaholic's feelings. The spouse feels and expresses the workaholic's emotions of happiness, sadness, frustration, anger, and hurt; since the workaholic is usually completely out of touch with his own feelings. Even if the workaholic begins to recognize his emotions, the spouse will come in on cue and assume the emotions for him so he won't be hurt. The spouse takes away the workaholic's feelings and thus can control his moods and happiness. For example, "Jane" thought she controlled her workaholic husband's feelings. She wanted to have a pleasant, responsibility-free evening with "Bill". Knowing that Bill would come home and feel pressured by all of the unfinished projects, Jane spent her entire afternoon mowing the lawn, trimming the bushes, cleaning the house, doing some laundry, making dinner - all the chores she could think of that would "keep" Bill from relaxing and enjoying the evening. When Bill called from work, she was excited to tell him all that she had accomplished. Bill was delighted by the news because he said "this freed him

<u>Notes</u>

up to stay at work for a late meeting." Needless to say, Jane was hurt and angered by this, but chose not to express her feelings to Bill. She is a "people-pleaser". People pleasers don't want others mad at them, so they don't express their anger to other because they're afraid that others will "go away" from them either emotionally or physically. By the time Bill arrived home, he was too tired from working long hours to enjoy his wife. Jane was too angry and hurt to be with Bill, so they spent the evening apart; neither sharing any feelings, nor trying to resolve the problem. Too many of these situations will produce resentful people, thereby damaging the intimacy and destroying the relationship little by little.

The workaholic's spouse assumes the role of caretaker for the workaholic's emotions. Our friend, Jane, blames the Corporation for "keeping him for late meetings" or for "working him so hard during the day that he doesn't have any energy left for his family", rather than holding Bill accountable and responsible for his own decisions. Jane's anger towards the Corporation frees Bill from feeling any of his own anger towards himself or the Corporation. Most of the time, the enabling spouse feels guilty for not being "enough" of a wife for the workaholic. Jane doesn't realize that she is not responsible for anyone's unhappiness except her own.

If Bill is also a perfectionist, there would never be anything she could do that would be "good enough". Jane gets the impression she can control Bill's moods, because Bill has falsely led her to that belief. He releases his anger onto the family through blame for reasons like, "she doesn't have dinner

Notes

ready, the children are too loud, the house is a mess, there's not enough money", and the list continues. Neither Jane or Bill hold Bill accountable for his own moods. If Jane accepts the theory that she is to blame and therefore responsible, then she will continue to try to control everything and everyone around her that might "cause" the workaholic to get angry.

The enabling spouse might even be the subject of the children's anger. The children might accept the workaholic's theory that "Mom" is at fault. Believing this, the children may get angry at Mom for "allowing" his moods to infect their household, thereby dictating the atmosphere of the entire house. We'll return to Jane and Bill's family to illustrate this point.

Prior to Bill coming home from work one night, Jane and their sons, Adam (7) and Jesse (4), were playing around, laughing, and having a terrific evening. Bill came home from work agitated. When he walked into the laughter-filled room where the rest of the family was, he barked off some comments about how the day had gone for him and said something about the laughter being to loud in the room. Precisely at that moment, their two sons stopped laughing, went downstairs, and began coloring very quietly in their coloring books. Jane, also, quietly went downstairs and began fixing dinner. The entire atmosphere of the house was allowed to change just by the mere presence of Dad, the workaholic. Everyone took their cues from Dad and changed their behavior, as if forced to assume responsibility for Dad's bad mood. One person had enough power to change the attitudes of three others. Given enough of these situations, patterns of unhealthy relationships develop, as it has with Jane

Notes

and Bill's family. Once again, it would be easy to place full blame on either Bill or Jane. However, we know that difficulties in relationships are equally created and each has contributed to this pattern of response to each other. Everyone's denial of their feelings clearly enables this pattern to continue.

Another way the spouse enables workaholism is through believing the words of the workaholic, while ignoring his behavior and actions. When words give one message and actions give a contradictory message, the enabler desperately wants to believe the words being spoken. For example, Bill often tells Jane that he loves her and that he places top priority on their marriage and family. If she were to pay attention to only the non-verbal behavior, she would receive another message, loud and clear. She would see that he works a 60-hour week, rarely stopping for lunch or breaks, being unwilling to take time off from work for himself or his family, traveling a great deal without rest in between trips, bringing work home every night, missing planned family activities, etc. Jane frustrates herself by being conscious, at some level of both messages being given. What gives the truer, clearer messages are the non-verbal behaviors. Bill's intention sounds nice and is desired - saying that he wants to be home with the family - but the result of his behavior, the consequences of his choices, with not enhance intimacy and will create a separation from the family.

If the enabling spouse continues to deny her own feelings about how the workaholic's behavior has affected her, she will find that this develops into a pattern, or habit, of responding to

Notes

others. The situation becomes a prime breeding ground for unhealthy roles to emerge. In his book "Stage II Relationships", Earnie Larsen describes six patterns of behavior that are usually modeled to us in childhood. The bad news is that we learned these patterns and they have become hurtful in our relationships. The good news is that we can unlearn these patterns.

Earnie Larsen cautions that it doesn't mean we're a bad person if we practice these patterns.

The six learned patterns of behavior are Caretaker, Martyr, People-pleaser, Workaholic, Perfectionist, and Tap Dancer. Though much can be written on each, we will only briefly describe three of these patterns, and illustrate how they fit with the workaholic family.

The Caretaker's motto is, as Earnie Larsen writes, "I am responsible for all things and all people at all times". They force themselves onto others by insisting "on doing for others what other should do and need to do for themselves." In her book "Co-dependent No More", Melodie Beattie referred to the Caretakers as "Rescuers". She writes that they rescue people from their responsibilities, then later, get mad at them for doing all they have done. Our friend, Jane, is a Caretaker. She has chosen to feel responsible for Bill's happiness or unhappiness. She has been choosing to make sure things are "just right" at the time Bill returns home from work, and tries to control or assume responsibility for his moods. She is rescuing him when she tries to think of ways for him to relieve his stress

<u>Notes</u>

after a hard day. It is Bill's responsibility to do this for himself. Jane takes away the opportunity for Bill to learn what he would like to do. It needs to be Bill's choice, and in his control alone to become aware of his needs and ways to meet those needs. Jane is rescuing Bill when she tells the children not to be angry with Daddy because he missed having lunch with Adam at school due to an unscheduled meeting. In this case, four messages are given: Adam has no right to his feelings, that he shouldn't express them, that his feelings aren't important, and that Daddy can't handle negative feelings from others. None of these messages are true. There are probably thousands of ways Jane rescued Bill. If this relationship has become to painful and Jane wanted to change it, we know that changing herself first is the healthiest way to induce change. Earnie Larsen suggest asking, "Where did your partner learn that it was acceptable to act in such a manner? "How long has he, or she, been able to get away with it?", and "What will this person lose if he won't change?". Remembering that people will not change if they're not uncomfortable will lead Jane to look at Bill's comfort level. She can always invite him to change by changing herself first.

The second pattern of behavior that we often find in a workaholic situation is the People-pleaser. Earnie Larsen states that these people "have never learned to say no. If they say no, they think others would get mad at them; and when that happens, it means they're bad people and would be abandoned by the people they love." These are the ones who say that everything is "just fine" when they're really feeling that their whole world is falling apart. Again, let's look at Bill and Jane's situation.

Notes

Jane was a people pleaser throughout her life. As the 4th child, her true needs were very seldom considered, and her desires were not known. She was overshadowed by her older brothers' needs and personalities. Once married to Bill, those same conditions were repeated in the early years of marriage. Bill was also a people pleaser, being an only child, shy, and needing the support and recognition of others. He had not learned how to say "No", and say "This is what I need or want". As time went on, Bill's need to please Jane, in order to maintain their marriage, took him to places where he did not want to go, or feel comfortable going, emotionally. Bill was a "white hat" guy, just as Jane was a "white hat" gal. Both were trying to please each other, and the people around them, while most of the time they both were very uncomfortable, sad, or pained inside. As a result, neither was being honest with the other partner during their marriage. True feelings were not shared, and each was living a life solely for the security and comfort of the other. Though physical abuse was never an issue, emotional abuse, shown more in the interpersonal actions, was very prevalent. As time went on, the daily conversations were almost exclusively about household business and child raising. The interpersonal thoughts and feelings were not discussed in an attempt to resolve the downward spiraling relationship, leading to disaster.

The final pattern for discussion is the "Perfectionist". Earnie Larsen states: "The perfectionist's self-image is based on doing things 'well enough'. Unfortunately, to the perfectionist 'well enough' means 'perfectly'. But since nothing on earth is perfect, perfectionists are locked in a terrible cycle of always

Notes

having to do better." This pattern fits our friend, Bill, to a "T". Bill, as an only child, and a "people pleaser", tried so hard as a child to draw praise from his father. Bill's father had been physically and emotionally abused as a child by his father, and as such, did not learn the parenting skills to show praise to his son, Bill. Bill's father also had lived a life along the "road of the school of hard knocks". Being permanently suspended from school because of his refusal to change from being left-handed, Bill's father was a common sense type of person, and learned various trades to survive and support his family. To rise through the ranks of his jobs to financially support his family, he became a perfectionist. This was Bill's role model for success. As a child, Bill's projects always had to be "perfect" in his father's eyes, or his father would take them over to provide Bill with the best that he could offer. As an example, one day Bill was building a tree house out of scrap lumber. It was a fine tree house for an 8-year old child, and Bill was pleased. But for Bill's father, it was not "perfect". Bill's father bought new lumber, tore down Bill's attempt, and rebuilt a much grander tree house, which Bill seldom used. Similar events happened with Bill's model train set, push carts, etc. This process showed Bill that if he wanted praise and recognition for his attempts and accomplishments, rather than criticism, he had to be "perfect" in all he attempted. Though most projects and efforts were not "perfect" throughout his life, Bill always thought he had to achieve perfection to receive recognition from his parents, his spouse, his children, his superiors, his co-workers, and his friends. Even after the death of his father, who created this perfection-oriented goal in Bill's inner self, Bill continued to self critique all his efforts, always trying to obtain perfection in the

Notes

material values which seemed so important. Bill never tried to achieve the same perfection in the spiritual and emotional relationships with his spouses, because he was taught that material values were more important.

The other patterns of behavior described in "Stage II Relationships", include "The Martyr", "The Workaholic", and "The Tap Dancer". Since this book focuses on "The Workaholic", this pattern have not been discussed specifically in this chapter. As our family with Bill and Jane does not have "The Martyr" and "The Tap Dancer" behavior patterns as prevalent as the others already discussed, the writer has chosen not to include them in this chapter.

Each individual may enable workaholism, or workaholic tendencies, in their daily life to some degree. It is the magnitude of that degree which makes the big difference, and the ability of the individual to adjust, or control, their lifestyle and the impact on those surrounding the workaholic, that is important to self-evaluate.

Notes

Chapter 5 - God and Trust

This chapter describes a presentation which was used at a Discovery Weekend at my Episcopal church in July, 1992. The emotional effects of the experiences which surround the activities which occurred just prior to the events in January, 1992, which will be related still effect my health and daily life.

As part of my recovery program, I developed a very strong awareness of the direct relationship between workaholism and codependency. I wish to share the events which occurred from January 25, 1992 through the next few months.

It was a typical weekend, towards the end of winter. We'd been cooped up too long in the house, and I especially, had cabin fever. My work schedule, as I review my daily calendar had been difficult as usual. I was still putting in 50 to 60 hours each week. It was Saturday morning and Janey had gone to flute practice to prepare for an upcoming event with the church, Discovery Weekend, on February 1st. As usual, I had brought home some work to try and catch up on. I heard the boys upstairs doing boy stuff. Loud screams and arguing from siblings, it was too much. This distraction from my work was angering me as I continued to loose my concentration. I ran

Notes

upstairs in a rage and "blasted" the boys for making too much noise and disturbing me. In a letter to the boys which I wrote on the following Monday I stated, "I see the anger which you see in my face and hear in my voice. I wish a hundred times over that I can remove that from your memories - not only last night but all the nights and days before. I truly hope my desire to learn a different way will be fulfilled."

When Janey returned, she was greeted by two very hurt and unhappy children. As the day proceeded not much was discussed until the boys went to bed that evening. Adam has the ability to talk with Janey. A talent I have yet to acquire.

Adam related the incidents of the day and expressed to Janey the hurt and fear which both he and Jesse felt from me. Janey understood the scenario, as we had played it so many times before. This was finally the time for a change. After a few hours of discussion, we mutually agreed it would be most beneficial for me to leave the house until I was able to handle my anger and rage.

I packed the car that evening, not knowing if I would be able to return. I have always had a problem with control. I must be in control at all times, and the thought of opening myself up to someone else, a stranger, a counselor, was very fearful. I drove around for quite some time trying to figure out where to go. I returned to the house three times before I realized this was serious and a real decision. I finally found a motel and settled in for the night.

Notes

My emotions were at extremes that night and for many to come. I took my Codependents Anonymous (CODA) materials and read and re-read. I prayed a lot to my Higher Power - GOD, to ask for his help in my recovery as well as support for my family. I had finally hit the bottom and I knew that I must work at recovery so I could return to my family.

I stayed in the motel for several nights before I figured out who I could ask for help. Jesse's godfather has always been a good friend and I called to ask if I could stay with him for awhile. "No problem, glad to have the company." What a wonderful feeling to have some refuge from the cold, cruel world, created mostly by obsessive people like myself.

I began therapy the very next day following my move out of the house. It was difficult at first and my engineering logic didn't compute the problems which I was having. I put my trust in GOD to see me through, each hour of each day. I continued with therapy once and sometimes twice a week. We also had family sessions to get a full picture of my addictive behavior.

On February 12, 1992, between 9PM and 10PM I had a long telephone conversation with Janey while I was in Little Rock, Arkansas.

We began the conversation with pleasantries and light issues, but quickly the conversation again turned to the single focus of when I would or could return home.

Notes

I stated again that I thought my awareness of my anger was in a state in which I could return. My desire, though not verbally stated, was to return the following Saturday.

As we continued to talk, Janey spoke of other concerns which she had not seen me address. Janey was very cautious of her selection of words, as she felt she may be doing some of my work again. However, I tried to assure her that what I was trying to get was information. This whole personality and behavior stuff is so foreign to me, like a baby, who has never been exposed to certain ideas. Janey spoke of her concerns that I have a very limited infrastructure of friends to turn to when I get into a crisis. I have none. I rely on my work and then Janey, Adam and Jesse.

After we hung up I got ready for bed, but about 11PM I began to toss and turn. I began to have a severe pain in the middle of my chest and heartburn really bad. As I lay there I began to think that this is my bad "memory boards" inside that are really getting upset. As I examined it again I began to see very painful parallels between the conversation I had with Janey and one of the final conversations I had with Denise before I made the decision to divorce Denise. Though I don't remember the particulars, I remember very vividly the desire for Denise to change me into someone I wasn't.

The longer I lay in bed the more I feared that Janey was also wanting to remold me into a person who she wanted and not the person who I am. I asked GOD all night to remove the pain from my chest and bring the light of his healing to me. To get

Notes

rid of the bad "memory boards" of my personality and replace them with ones which will allow me to live the rest of my life with my family.

I decided the next morning that I did want to come home <u>now</u>, but I want to also develop the necessary personality behavior memory patterns so I don't backslide. It hurts too much to be away now. I decided to let GOD handle that one.

It is now six months later. I returned home about the first of March, 1992, and we've really done pretty well. We do more things as a family, I have tried to do more in creating relationships with my friends so I have an outlet. In March we had a major layoff at work and I had to let several, and one particularly close friend go. I have had a severe physical reaction to all this with the loss of four layers of skin on my hands, severe cracking of the skin on my feet, loss of feeling in my fingers, a muscle spasm in the muscle under my left breast and sometimes dizziness. I have had a complete physical and have been declared "healthy as a horse". The stress of potentially losing my family from this incident and the stress of having to layoff my friends has just about done me in. Without my trust in GOD and my belief that he is watching out for me each and every moment of the day, I probably would not survive. I truly believe the poem about "Footprints in the Sand". He has carried me through some of the most difficult moments in my life.

Notes

Chapter 6 - Benefits of Workaholism

Oh, the benefits! The glorious, often destructive, often deadly benefits of being a workaholic. Let's examine what the benefits are of being a workaholic and to whom or what the majority of the benefits are received.

By far the greatest recipient of the benefits from the workaholic is the Corporation. Who better to receive the benefit of intense productivity, generally without having to reimburse the workaholic. Why? In general the workaholic would be a professional or a manager or a supervisor - a "white collar worker", who is not required to be compensated on an overtime basis for extra hours on the job. The Corporation therefore receives the bottom-line profit which is generated by the workaholic, whether it is from extra hours of planning a project, to compulsive work habits which result in extra widgets. The Corporation also benefits from the workaholic because the subordinates of the workaholic supervisor, whether knowingly or unknowingly, will tend to follow the lead of their supervisor and "put in a little extra" without documenting the time or effort, to be praised by their supervisor. Recognition for a job well done, especially in the economic restructuring times of the 90's, with downsizing and layoffs in every industry, is extremely

Notes

important. That workaholic project manager, department manager or supervisor does have some power to decide on the workers future. Subconsciously the worker wants the praise of his or her superior, the recognition of doing a better than average job, and the "security" that if a downsizing does occur, that workaholic supervisor will be on their side when the pink slips begin to be distributed. But who really benefits from this cycle - the Corporation.

In my own case, I was a senior project manager, and an executive for an engineering company. I had approximately 40 employees in my engineering group of all engineering disciplines and technical levels of skills. Though I am a workaholic, I try very consciously not to directly impose my addiction on my people. They all know I am a workaholic, because we have had a group session in which I discussed my addiction. I try to be fair and unbiased when completing their annual evaluations and recommendations for salary adjustments. Am I successful? I know that some of my non-exempt employees put in more than 40 hours per week and do not request overtime. I also know that these same people have personal needs at times and do not run "by the clock", which generally balances out their extra effort. I do know that for many the experience and excitement which we try to create does have many putting in extra time, which is billed to our clients and not directly compensated to the employee, the resulting beneficiary - the Corporation.

Is this so bad? Our employees are not unhappy, they have as steady an income as can be provided in this day and age

Notes

and in general, if asked, they would probably say everything is OK. In the eyes of God we are exploiting these persons in some small way and therefore, I personally, as an upper level management employee, do not always uphold all the corporate regulations when dealing with my group, just because I do not believe all our regulations are morally correct. I try to treat my fellow workers with the dignity they deserve as respective human beings. They are good people, they do work hard. They do not work in an addictive manner, and as part of my recovery process I believe it is my responsibility to not encourage workaholism, even though the Corporation will benefit from this type of behavior. I suggest that as you read this book you review your own situation, whether you are a supervisor or an employee. You should treat or be treated in the way you believe is morally proper.

How do the enablers benefit from the workaholic? Certainly not as much as the Corporation. Those who enable the workaholic are probably those who know and love the workaholic the most- family, friends, neighbors and business relations. As these people watch the workaholic go about his or her way of life, the enablers do receive some benefits, many projects which are completed around the house, a nice house, car and perks from the compensation which the workaholic receives from the Corporation and usually a devoted spouse. The workaholic is probably not one to "run around" on his or her spouse, though the workaholic does have a mistress - WORK, which will be discussed more in the next chapter.

Notes

For those of us who are workaholics the benefits are believed to be great. We are highly respected by our Corporation for the outstanding effort and commitment we make to the job. The recognitions we achieve, and the invitations to participate in different organizations are ego boosters. Our families do enjoy the nice cars, nice homes, country club perks, frequent flyer free tickets, etc.

Notes

Chapter 7 - Hazards of Workaholism

There are many hazards to being a workaholic, many of which will be discussed in this chapter. Being a workaholic it is not often easy to identify the hazards, so some of these will be identified by those close to those of us who have least acknowledged that we are workaholics.

By far the most noticeable hazard which is self-identifiable is our health. The problem with this hazard is our denial in the early stages of health problems. When a non-dysfunctional individual would immediately go to the doctor or dentist to receive medical treatment, the workaholic will not recognize that there is a problem which requires assistance. More commonly, there is work to be performed which has a deadline that can't be missed; therefore we put off our medical health needs. This is also of our mental health. Though we recognize that we do have a problem with addiction, especially workaholism, do we respond by calling a therapist or a psychologist -probably not!! In both of these types of health situations, I have had to have a severe incident before I tend to go to receive the medical treatment which is needed.

Notes

Another hazard is when the workaholic is in a supervisory position. The subordinate workers are subject to criticism of their work patterns, work ethics, productivity, etc. by the workaholic. Being in a management role, I have always tried to be sensitive of my expectations of those who work in my group or department. It is important that the workaholic supervisor have the ability to detach his or her expectations during employee appraisals, and compliment your employees on their accomplishments, even though you may believe you could have done more in a shorter time or could have performed multiple tasks as the same time.

The hazards of being a workaholic in a corporate environment involve the unrealistic expectations which can be created by the upper management of the corporation. At some time even the strongest workaholic will break down. Even though we believe we are "superhumans" when it comes to work, our physical constraints as human beings will not allow us to continue at the intense pace we usually operate at forever. The expectations of upper management are created by our initial efforts. Eventually we either "take a break" or recognize that our efforts are significantly greater than those of our peers, who usually are compensated at the same rate, and we say "take this job and shove it"! This then puts us in a bad light with upper management and they begin to overlook us for promotions, raises, perks, etc.

By far the greatest hazard is the destructive relationship with our families. There are several aspects which affect the workaholic, of which I will describe in more detail than the

Notes

previous hazards. As you read this, reflect upon your own family relationships, either past or present, to see how your workaholic behavior has affected your life and the life of your family.

One day my wife and I were discussing my workaholic "go, go, go" patterns, both at work and for those endless projects to be completed at home. She said "Do you realize all the details of our children's lives which you miss"? We discussed some of the details of our boys' activities and developmental stages, and I did not know most of them.

I find many times when I come home from work, I immediately walk into the house, say a brief hello, and proceed immediately to helping prepare dinner, or go to the computer to do some work, or go to the back yard to do some activity and the list goes on. Very seldom do we sit down and relax. "Relax" is not a word which seems to be in our vocabulary. When dinner is finished on my plate, I leave the table and begin to clean the cooking dishes, even if the rest of the family is still eating and even if I was involved in a conversation. This is not only discourteous and rude, but destroys any existing relationship or prohibits the development of a relationship with family members. My wife says that she doesn't want to share information with me, because I usually don't take time to listen or discuss.

The relationships with friends and family can be severely affected by the workaholic's behavior patterns. The workaholic is usually able to preplan a "project" in his mind and set that plan into action. If a friend or family member tries to intervene or

Notes

suggest alternative methods of accomplishing the project, the result may be a rude response from the workaholic. Though there is nothing wrong with the comment, it affects the "control" issue which the workaholic finds so precious. The responses usually initiated by the workaholic may include anger, sharp response tones in voice, physical distancing from the friend or family member, to total rejection of a relationship.

The relationship with our children, our most precious gift from God, is also severely impaired as workaholic. I find myself looking at my older son, now 11 years old, acting exactly as his Dad. As my father taught me, work comes first, then play. I, in turn, both consciously and subconsciously am doing the same to my sons. If all homework isn't done, my expectations are that they should not play or take a break until their homework is completely finished. Young people do not have the stamina to be workaholics, and they turn to drugs or suicide as an outlet for the expectations we place upon their minds. They are not able to cope with the pace. I find that to relax from homework, my oldest son goes out and does another work activity, rather than playing. I told my wife that she and I didn't see eye-to-eye on his following my instructions. I had told him to take a break from homework one weekend and not be dismantling a swing set. She told me, "your son looks to you for an example and when you sit down and relax, so will he and then I'll support your instructions to him". Frightening reality, eh! The old cliché "Do as I say, not as I do" is not applicable in the 90s. Our children are more independent and strong willed than we baby boomers were as children. Our society has created this principle.

Chapter 7 - Hazards of Workaholism

Notes

Being a workaholic does not allow me to turn off my engine and relax. My mind is going every waking moment as to the tasks which have yet to be done and planning when they will be performed. Whether its work related, church related, scout related, or family related my mind is always going. It is best described for me as the Wheel of Fortune wheel spinning. Wherever it stops there is a work task to be done right then and once completed the wheel spins again for another task. The wheel never stops. Many times my wife will say "Please spend a little time with me, both physically and mentally". Most times even if I sit down and am physically present, my mind is racing 1000 miles an hour as to what I should be doing, rather than sitting. It is a true curse to our family, for we miss so much of the beauty of the family and the interest of our spouse and children.

What's the "bottom line" on all of this chapter. As we continue to act in our workaholic behavior patterns, we affect not only our lives, but equally or greater, we affect the lives of those around us, including our superiors, our peers, our subordinates, and most of all our loved ones.

Notes

Chapter 8 - "So Now What" for the Workaholic

"So Now What", now that we have discovered what a Workaholic is, what a Workaholic does, how a Workaholic affects his or her and others lives. Let's take a look at some of the areas of where the workaholic can find support and how assistance for the workaholic can be provided for those who desire help.

Self-help groups - Resources are available for the workaholic in our society, but again remember that workaholism is the compulsion that is stroked by corporate America because they benefit from the behaviors of a workaholic. To date, Big Business has not been outwardly supportive of rehabilitation of the workaholic, and thus there is not a lot of financial or societal support for recovery from workaholism, as there is for alcoholism, drug addiction, child abuse, etc.

There are a few Workaholics Anonymous (WA) Groups in the United States, which primarily began on the East and West coasts in the larger cities. Being from the Mid-west, there are not any such WA chapters in the mid-section of the country. There are other support groups available, though which are not directly related to Workaholism, but more the fundamental source of the workaholic's issues. One such primary support

<u>Notes</u>

group is CODA - Codependents Anonymous. This support group relates more with the codependent behavior of an individual and their relationship with family and others.

As I reviewed my codependent behaviors in my CODA 12-Step program, I found that my workaholism was a direct result of codependency. As I worked my 6th Step I found many issues in my early childhood years that created my addiction to workaholism. My father was a workaholic, not so much by desire but by necessity of his upbringing and economic times during the Great Depression. As a result of his intense workaholic tendencies, the only recognition I remember receiving as a child from my father was for hard work and successful completion of projects.

Brainstorming with Family -The family unit can be a very helpful resources for the workaholic. From the youngest to the oldest, each member loves the workaholic and wants the person to remain a part of the family. Discussing the issues which create difficult feelings for the family members and the workaholic sometimes helps "clear the air" of anger, frustration and resentment feelings.

Family members can help the workaholic recognize that the workaholic is in one of his or her "whirlwinds" by using phrases which have been mutually developed and are not threatening to the workaholic. A gentle reminder such as "Count to ten for a minute"; "Daddy, take a look in the mirror"; "Would you like to take a walk"; etc. Very non-threatening phrases, yet a signal from the family members that the workaholic is doing his or

Notes

her thing and affecting the family. These are not intended to relieve the workaholic of his or her responsibilities for recovery, yet a supportive nudge because many times we are not able to recognize that we are in a whirlwind, especially in early periods of recovery.

<u>Brainstorming at Work</u> - Recognition at the workplace by the workaholic's supervisors, peers and subordinates of the triggers of workaholic behavior which affect the workaholic are extremely important. Sharing your recognition of workaholism with these individuals is an extremely humbling experience, yet one in which you are able to express your acknowledgment of your addictive behavior. Most of these individuals may already recognize that you are a workaholic or exhibit workaholic tendencies, even if they are not able to identify the addiction by name.

Again, as with the family, most individuals with whom you work do care about you as an individual and are willing to provide support and understanding, yet only after the workaholic initiates the process. Perhaps co-workers will offer to support some of the workload which the workaholic may have assumed, rather than delegating work responsibilities. Their offer of help is usually in a gesture of caring for you, so accept their offer with grace and thankfulness. Allow the gift of sharing to be accepted by both the individual who offers as well as you.

The workaholic begins to recognize that certain periods of time are extremely stressful, with signs such as when the muscles in your neck begin to ache with stress. Take care of yourself.

Notes

Whether it is time to take a 10-minute break and walk outside; close your office door and close your eyes and go to a safe place in your mind; or tell someone you need to take off for the afternoon; those around you who are aware of your situation will usually be supportive. Remember that if you are that stressed, you are probably not doing justice to the work you are performing. You are not effective, efficient or productive. You are only in a workaholic addictive cycle that keeps your mind going at an extremely rapid pace, without proper thought to your actual task at hand.

What are your expectations for recovery? As an identified and acknowledged workaholic, I believe that my expectations for recovery are very slim. I expect that I will be a workaholic for the rest of my life. However, I also believe that with a proper 12-Step program, a continuous recognition of my addiction and a loving, supportive family, I will be able to maintain my family, and my work. For me, it will be a 24/7, 365 days per year acknowledgment and recognition that I am a workaholic and that I need to "stay on the wagon". It is extremely difficult for a workaholic to be that aware of his or her behavior patterns. Promises of recovery do get made and do get broken, probably more so that any other addiction. The biggest success is for me in my recovery is for me to recognize that I need to stop a workaholic cycle and acknowledge to my family that I am in such a cycle, before a family member gets so fed up with my behavior that they have to intervene and tell me that I'm in another cycle.

Notes

The expectation that total recovery is possible is probably very unrealistic. The expectation that the workaholic is able to recognize behavior patterns and adjust behavior before destruction occurs to a relationship is a true success.

<u>Notes</u>

Chapter 9 - "So Now What" for the Enablers

Now that both the Workaholic and the Enablers are aware of the addiction and the effects of the addiction, what do the enablers do differently in their relationships with the workaholic. Though there are no real answers and there is no documented experience, this chapter will share some of the experiences of the writer, his family and friends.

The spouse is probably the best individual to begin this discussion. The outward recognition by both the workaholic and the spouse is a major step in improvement of the marital relationship. No longer does the spouse have to "tread lightly" around the workaholic and the disruptive behaviors found in the immediate family. The ability of the spouse to verbally express feelings to the workaholic empowers the spouse to not only feel stronger in the relationship, but also to verbally express displeasure when the workaholic is "racing" and affecting the immediate family members. The verbal expression by the spouse needs to be for the benefit of the spouse though, not as a crutch for the workaholic to recognize that it is time to start the recovery process - AGAIN!

Notes

The spouse has several choices in this relationship. One choice is to stay with the workaholic and be supportive during the recovery process, while knowing there will probably be many falls off the wagon and many broken promises. Another choice is for the spouse to leave the relationship, either on a temporary basis or on a permanent basis. This is certainly a major decision by the spouse, yet in instances where the workaholic is so ingrained in the addiction, the workaholic is probably never there either physically or mentally and the final separation may actually be a relief to the spouse. The spouse may also find relief in a 12-step program, similar to AL-ANON for enablers of Alcoholics. There may be some type of behavioral recognition which the spouse needs to examine and why they chose a workaholic for a spouse in the first place.

The children of the workaholic may also be enablers of the addition of the workaholic. Again, the educating of the children of the family may help the workaholic in recovery. The children need to be encouraged at an early age that the behaviors of the workaholic parent are not to be copied by example. As the spouse of the workaholic begins to recognize that a "mini-workaholic" is developing, the parents need to discuss the approach to "break the cycle". This may be a family approach, use of professional therapy or other ideas which some of the readers may have found to be successful. There are no right or wrong answers to these situations, whatever works is acceptable.

Open communication between family members which is not threatening to any of the individuals involved is the best

Notes

approach we have found to date. The support by professional therapists is a highly recommended part of the recovery and recognition for the workaholic and his or her family. Recovery from an addiction by an individual in the family unit affects each member of the family. Everyone will need to make some adjustments in daily behavior patterns. These patterns were created when the workaholic was not in recovery and the family members created a living pattern. When the workaholic is in recovery, the old patterns of living are probably no longer valid, thus each member needs to adjust their individual living patterns and the living patterns of the family as a whole.

Notes

Chapter 10 - "So Now What" for the Corporation

Well the biggest loser in the recovery of the workaholic is probably the Corporation. The corporation no longer receives all the intense production by the workaholic, no longer receives the financial compensation as a result of the workaholic patterns of the employee, and no longer has a leader who imposes either consciously or unconsciously their workaholic patterns on other employees in the corporation.

What will the corporation receive from the recovery of the workaholic. The recovering workaholic can be viewed as a resource in today's society as an individual who can assist the Corporation with savior of their most valuable asset - the employees who work for the corporation. When the corporation hires an individual and goes through the years of training and advancement of an individual, only to have them "burn out" just at the time they are the most valuable, the corporation has to start all over again. The recovering workaholic can help valuable employees divert from "burn out". Who better to help employees moderate their work behaviors than an individual who has been on the edge. In Japan, the rate of suicide has increased dramatically in the early 90s, much from workaholic stress. The corporations in Japan are investigating ways to

<u>Notes</u>

reduce stress in the workplace, again because they see before their eyes their most valuable resource being destroyed.

The recovering workaholic can work with fellow employees and create a support group, in the corporate environment to relieve stress, discuss everyday work problems by brainstorming ideas that could lead to solutions which could improve the corporation.

The corporation and the individual workers need to be able to distinguish between being a hard worker and a workaholic. There is nothing wrong with working hard, for that individual must have a feeling of accomplishment at the end of each and every day. For most workers, the corporation is the place where they spend most of their productive years. They must be satisfied with that environment and with their accomplishments.

However, those who remain workaholics, and are unable or unwilling to proceed along the path of recovery, will continue to be benefits, though perhaps short term to the Corporation. These workers will continue to put in long hours, generally without compensation, for the benefit of the Corporation. One day though, the sacrifices that have benefited the Corporation will come crashing down. Either the workaholic will totally burn out at work, stress out at work due to overwhelming workload and frustration, or will physically no longer be able to perform, either through stroke, heart attack, or death.

Notes

Chapter 11 - The Power of the Holy Spirit

During the period of recovery, the most important and exciting benefit was the renewal of my faith in God and the Holy Spirit. This has made a substantial change in the focus of my life. Though the recovery from Workaholism was ineffective for a period of time as discussed in Chapter 12 of this book, the renewal of the power of the Holy Spirit now leads my daily life.

I have always believed in God and the Holy Spirit, but now listen intently to the messages which I believe are given to me through times of quiet meditation, and by asking God for help in times of need. Concurrently, I continue to praise God for all the gifts which He gives me each day, and am much more aware of these gifts.

During my period of recovery and counseling, I became much closer to my church, both in worship and serving the needs of the church and others. My service is also done in a very humble manner, seeking no recognition or rewards. I have learned the deep satisfaction of giving to others, expecting nothing in return.

Notes

One day during counseling with my assistant priest we went into the sanctuary, and kneeled at the base of the altar. There I was placed into a spiritual cleansing, and while my mind went from a blackness into the white light of God, unknown and uncontrolled, I reached up my arms to the Lord, and wept uncontrollably, asking God for forgiveness for all my sins, especially for my workaholic addiction, and the hurt which had been borne upon my wife and children. I asked for God's blessing which I believe was touched upon my forehead. This was such an extraordinary experience, and will be clearly remembered all the remaining days of my life.

Now, as I sit in our sanctuary, I have a much greater sense of the Holy Spirit during our worship services. I believe the Lord's angels are present, smiling down on our congregation. Each time the sun shines brightly upon the altar and upon the congregation, I smile, knowing that the Holy Spirit is with us.

We all have goals which we desire to achieve in our lifetimes, and one of my goals is to always be a humble servant of the Lord. I continue to serve as a Lay Reader and Lay Eucharistic Minister in the Episcopal Church. One day, I would like to be ordained as a Deacon in the Church. Several have asked if I desire to be an Episcopal priest. Yes, this also would be a desire, but the education requirements seem overwhelming at this time. Perhaps in time and with God's help one of these goals will be achieved.

The strong desire to serve the Lord is always with me. I have come to believe that the engineering training I received

Notes

years ago, and have practiced for over 30 years, was given to me by God to use for the benefit of my fellow man. This has helped during periods of stressful events in my work, and has given my strength to move through these stressful events, into resolution or compromise on various issues with clients, contractors, manufacturers, peer employees, etc.

The most wonderful gift that the Holy Spirit has blessed me with is the continued wonderful relationship with my sons and a renewed relationship with my daughter. I thank God each day for these wonderful young people whose lives I try to shape, strongly encouraging family values and priority. My continuous comment is "Do as I say, not as I do. Do not follow in my path and turn out to be a workaholic like Dad." I love my children with all my heart, and try my best to set our special time together with priority. Not always accomplished, but always attempted.

<u>Notes</u>

Chapter 12 – So it this the End?

And now, its time to determine if this is the End.

After 17 years in my second marriage, we mutually agreed that it was better to end our marriage harmoniously, and perhaps return to the friendship with which we began our relationship. Though both saddened by our decision, it was if a large weight was taken from both our shoulders, and enlighten our lives. Our focus was on maintaining the least disruptive environment for our boys, regardless of the sacrifices which we may to personally endure. Though difficult, we managed to maintain our goals throughout the divorce procedure, with financial sacrifices made as necessary. We took both boys to counselors to help them through the process, and were very open with them about the need for this decision.

Today, three years later following the divorce, I remain single, and without any significant other, that is other than my "mistress" - Work!! My second wife has remarried the assistant priest who helped me during my period of attempted recovery from workaholism. My second wife has achieved the spiritual companionship which she desired and needed, we continue to

Notes

have a good friendship, and talk several times each week, not only about the boys, but also about things friends share.

I continue to share with my sons, the difficulties which I face as a result of being a workaholic, and hope they will hear what I say, and not do as I do.

I accept my addiction as a workaholic, and I will say that I really do enjoy my lifestyle. I have moved to the country, I am building a house for the boys and myself. I enjoy carpentry work, and have many other plans which will keep my addiction occupied. My friends support me and provide the interaction which I need, my church services provide me the spiritual fullness that I need, my active involvement with the Boy Scouts serves the outdoors and youthfulness that I desire, the benefits which my company receives are welcomed by them, and so life as a workaholic, at least for me, is OK.

I have made a commitment not to marry again. I believe that my choice of lifestyle, and that's what it is - a choice, should not harm any other persons again. There has been to much hurt to others who I loved because of my lifestyle. I truly believe that the Holy Spirit is with me always, so I am never alone. Over the past three years, there has been very few times when I have ever felt lonely, perhaps only on a weekend when the boys are not with me, does the house seem a little empty, and a little to quiet. When those times come, there's always a project to do, or company work to do, which will quickly fill that void. This seems to be the mark of a dedicated workaholic.

Notes

I do not recommend this lifestyle to all, but I will say, that for some of us, perhaps it is an acceptable lifestyle. I accept that I am a high risk for an early death, but I also believe that I have lived a very full life each day, and I believe that I have done God's work to serve my fellow human beings with the benefits of the gifts and talents which God has bestowed upon me.

I thank you for allowing me to share my outlook on the compulsion of being a workaholic. Perhaps reading this book will help others to continue on their road to recovery, or for some of us, find and accept a lifestyle in which it is acceptable to pronounce - I'm a workaholic and its OK.

Chapter 13 - The Rest of the Story

I have always enjoyed listening to Paul Harvey's "The Rest of the Story" on the radio. It has been almost ten years since I last worked on my book, and there is a lot to tell. So this chapter is the brief version of the "Rest of My Story".

The development of this chapter and the rest of my life are intertwined in several ways so be patient as I write this chapter almost 18 years after I began the book. In the last chapter I shared with you that I would never get married again – that changed. The workaholism that I have been writing about over the past 18 years related to corporate structure – that changed. I have always been a "Believer", but now I am on the road to being an "Active Believer" – that changed. And so now my life is much different now than when I left you in Chapter 12.

I remained single for over 4 years, continuing on my workaholic path in "Corporate America". The strokes were good. I bought land in the countryside to start a new life as a single person. I built a small house and had my boys with me on weekends when I was not traveling throughout the world. But something was missing. The loneliness and aloneness eventually got too much. I tried dating some of the women that I knew from work,

Notes

since that was the only place, other than church, that I knew anyone. But that was not very successful because of our long friendships that would not result in relationships. Internet dating was not my style.

Then one day in late 1999, and I don't remember now the circumstances, our receptionist caught my eye. We had been acquaintances through work, and our relationship was very business-like. I asked Vernessa to help me shop for Christmas gifts for my children before Christmas and we had dinner afterwards. She was quiet and a big help, but didn't seem to be interested in a relationship.

The new century and the new millennium occurred on January 1st without incident – the world did not come to an end. I was traveling a lot internationally at the time. Vernessa and I would talk once in a while. As I was leaving on one trip she walked me out to the parking lot on her break. I remember it as clearly today as if it happened yesterday. She wished me a safe trip and kissed me lightly on the lips – Wow! We both seemed a little stunned because we had been developing more of a friendship relationship rather than a romantic relationship. I returned from spring break with the kids. Vernessa and I had dinner again, took a day trip to Eureka Springs. While on yet another trip I said "I love you". She replied "I love you too." We talked about that and she said she was surprised that those words came from her mouth. She had been single for over 20 years after an abusive marriage. She had raised her only son by herself.

<u>Notes</u>

Quick version - we started dating, I asked her to marry my on May 2nd, we got her ring on May 5th, and we flew to Las Vegas on June 17th and got married. No one at the office knew but two of our closest friends. We set a "formal" wedding date on October 7th to have the wedding performed by her brother and later had a blessing ceremony at my church on December 7th. We celebrate each of these dates, each month, to thank God for bringing us together. We grow together more each day, each month, each year. We have been happily married for almost 7 years as I write this and we look forward to being together forever.

At the end of 2000, I had finished a series of Projects that I had been working with one client on for over 20 years. The "corporate" management asked me what I wanted to do next. Their response to my response was "We don't work in those countries". My response was "I guess you don't need me anymore". I have always really liked the song "Take this job and shove it" and that was my verbal reality version of that song. Fortunately, the sale of our original company and the stock that I had been presented over the years as bonuses for all my hard "workaholic" work permitted me the luxury of starting my own business. I have been self-employed for over seven years now and truly have enjoyed almost every moment. But this was the biggest change in my attitude towards work. There is an extreme difference between "working hard" and being a "workaholic". For over twenty-five years I was a workaholic – trying to please the corporate world and be rewarded with these luxuries of being a workaholic. Now I just work hard. This may be hard for people to understand, but there is a big

Notes

difference. Before, I was not only taken up physically by work, but also mentally. Now it is a physical taking by putting in a lot of long hours to serve my clients. I have no employees, except my wife who is a "partner" in the firm. She has learned to help with computer modeling, clerical, office management and marketing/advertising. We work together as a team. She understands my need to work hard and long hours. I understand her need to have me stop periodically and be with her - to sit together, to watch TV, to walk in the woods, to travel together, to laugh, to smile, to share, etc. It is easier now because I only report to God.

Our workload has grown over the years, so we built a new office/house in the woods. It was a lot of work, but we did it together and enjoy it together. That is another book in itself – but it would not have happened without our wonderful relationship, the support of each other, and the Blessings from God.

The best part of "The Rest of Story" is my growth and understanding of my relationship with my Creator. My belief in God was cultivated and developed early in my life with the help of my mother. The best way I can describe this relationship as I reflect over the past years is like I have been in a spiritual hibernation for most of my life. It is like a blossoming of the most wonderful relationship that can occur in this life. In the beginning of my marriage to Vernessa, I struggled between the two relationships, but I have come to understand that they are intertwined and my relationship would not be a wonderful without my relationship with my Savior Jesus. Vernessa was the daughter of a Pastor, one of eight children, and has both a

<u>Notes</u>

brother and sister who are Pastors. She has helped me blossom in my spiritual life. The church that I used to attend provided me with a theological base, but not the ability to praise and worship God and His Son in the manner that has been penned up inside of me. This blossoming, through the support of my wife and my sister-in-law who is our Pastor, has allowed me to view life with a totally different perspective and created new and wonderful relationships. I understand now and believe now that God is the most wondrous, awesome being that is in my life. Without God I would not be who I am or where I am today. I have read the Bible from front to back and now I am beginning a detailed study of the Book of Job. I enjoyed Job's story more than any book in the Bible. I look back and see some parallels in my life and Job's. I have never lost faith in God through all my trials and tribulations. I certainly was not as faithful as Job in the past, but I will be in the future.

Over these past years I have learned the following:

1. Never say Never
2. Trust in God, He will never leave you or forsake you
3. Be thankful for each day, it is not promised to us
4. Serve God faithfully and His blessings will abound
5. Do not take anything for granted, it is a Blessing from God
6. Miracles do exist
7. Take time to smell the flowers, watch the birds, listen to all of God's Creation, view all of the beauty that exists – both inside and outside of yourself
8. Be thankful and thank your spouse for the love that

Notes

you share each day

9. Love your children and grandchildren and take time to be with them
10. Listen, Listen, Listen – Don't always speak
11. Don't always try to fix things in your life or others – sometimes those things are there for a reason
12. There is a life other than the corporate life that we all live or "used to live"

I love life, enjoy life, and look forward to living a long and healthy life both physically and spiritually. I am not afraid of death because I know that a better life is ahead of me for all Eternity. But I am not ready yet to be with Jesus, because there is still a lot I want to do in this life. But I am starting to make a list of questions to sit with Him and ask when He calls me to return to His House.

I have a few words of wisdom for those reading this book. The major result of workaholism is divorce. A successful marriage is not easy under the best of conditions. Each party to a marriage needs to be aware of each other each day, all day long. A good marriage is a lot of work, and that is why our divorce rate is climbing each year. People are working at their jobs and don't want to work at their marriages. Each day is a commitment to the marriage vows, and the focus of a marriage is each other – not the children, not the finances, not the work, not the house, etc. The hardest thing we do as human beings is communicate, and a successful marriage requires good communication. That is first and foremost. It is also necessary to share the tasks of living together- share the

134

Notes

Chapter 13 - The Rest of the Story

big and little tasks. When one of the partners in a marriage has an issue, there are no big and small issues – each is as important as another.

Finally, the spouse of a professional (doctor, engineer, attorney, etc.) needs to understand our commitments and responsibilities to our clients. We serve people. There are strange time commitments, stress, liabilities, difficult work situations, and the list goes on and on. That is who we are and what we do. There are other professions that require hard work, but not all the pressures –primarily mentally - that we are required to withstand. It is important for the professionals to share their work life with their spouse (considering confidentialities) so the spouse knows and understands and can support the professional. This is not always easy. It is also important for the professional to understand the spouse who may be caring for the house, raising the children and a "bazillion" other things each day with an equal, though different type of stress, tiredness, shortness of attitude, etc. This comes back to the communication issue. Stay cool, calm, and collected. Leave your angers at the doorstep. You are a team working together.

I hope that you have enjoyed and learned from this short story. Over the years I shared my working manuscript with several couples that were having marriage problems because of work and workaholic tendencies. So far there is a 100 percent success rating in saving marriages. I hope this will work for you.

<u>Notes</u>

My last humble and sincere desire is to ask forgiveness of those who I have hurt over the years as a result of my Workaholism. There was never a day that went by that my desire was to hurt any of you, only to support you in the best way that I knew how. I now realize that the way I was going about it was wrong, but I did the best that I could.

God Bless Each of You

APPENDIX

FOOTNOTE SLOGANS

"Work Smarter, Not Harder"

"The Hard Work Begins after 5"

"When is it my turn?"

12 STEPS FOR A WORKAHOLIC

1. *We admitted we were powerless over work - that our lives had become unmanageable.*

   Promise: We are going to know a new freedom and a new happiness.

2. *Came to believe that a Power greater than ourselves could restore us to sanity.*

   Promise: We will not regret the past nor wish to shut the door on it.

3. *Made a decision to turn our will and our lives over to the care of God as we understood him.*

   Promise: We will comprehend the word serenity and we will know peace.

4. *Made a searching and fearless moral inventory of ourselves.*

   Promise: No matter how far down the scale we have gone, we will see how our experiences can benefit others.

5. *Admitted to God, to ourselves, and to another human being the exact nature of our wrongs.*

   Promise: The feeling of uselessness and self-pity will disappear.

6. Were entirely ready to have God remove all these defects of our character.

   Promise: We will lose interest in selfish things and gain interest in our fellows.

7. *Humbly asked Him to remove our shortcomings.*

   Promise: Self-seeking will slip away.

8. Made a list of all persons we had harmed, and became willing to make amends to them all.

   Promise: Our whole attitude and outlook upon life will change.

9. *10. Made direct amends to such people wherever possible, except when to do so would injure them or others.*

   Promise: Fear of people and of economic insecurity will leave us.

11. *Continued to take personal inventory and when we were wrong promptly admitted it.*

    Promise: We will intuitively know how to handle situations which use to baffle us.

12. *Sought through prayer and meditation to improve our conscious contact with God as we understand Him, praying only for knowledge of His will for us and the power to carry that out.*

    Promise: We will suddenly realize that God is doing for us what we could not do for ourselves.

13.   *Having had a spiritual awakening as the result of these steps, we tried to carry this message to workaholics and to practice these principles in all our affairs.*

Are these extravagant promises? We think not. They are being fulfilled among us - sometimes quickly, sometimes slowly. They will always materialize if we work for them.

-Author Unknown

www.ingramcontent.com/pod-product-compliance
Lightning Source LLC
Chambersburg PA
CBHW061306280526
45784CB00002B/916